BIGFOOT AND YETI

by Jennifer Joline Anderson

Content Consultant
Michael Delahoyde, PhD
Washington State University

CORE
LIBRARY

Published by ABDO Publishing Company, PO Box 398166, Minneapolis, MN 55439. Copyright © 2014 by Abdo Consulting Group, Inc. International copyrights reserved in all countries. No part of this book may be reproduced in any form without written permission from the publisher. The Core Library™ is a trademark and logo of ABDO Publishing Company.

Printed in the United States of America,
North Mankato, Minnesota
102013
012014

♲ THIS BOOK CONTAINS AT LEAST 10% RECYCLED MATERIALS.

Editor: Lauren Coss
Series Designer: Becky Daum

Library of Congress Cataloging-in-Publication Data
Anderson, Jennifer Joline, author.
  Bigfoot and Yeti / by Jennifer Joline Anderson.
     pages cm. -- (Creatures of legend)
  Includes index.
  Audience: 8 to 12.
  ISBN 978-1-62403-150-2
1. Sasquatch--Juvenile literature. 2. Yeti--Juvenile literature. I. Title.
  QL89.2.S2A53 2014
  001.944--dc23
                              2013027406

Photo Credits: AP Images, cover, 1, 16, 30, 45; Shutterstock Images, 4, 12 (left), 12 (center), 12 (center right), 15, 42; Thinkstock, 6, 12 (right); imagebroker/Alamy, 10; Rachisan Alexandra/Shutterstock Images, 12 (center left); Red Line Editorial, 12 (main), 23, 43 (top); Barry Lewis/ In Pictures/Corbis, 18; Mary Evans Picture Library/Alamy, 22; Malcolm Chandler/DK Images, 24, 43 (bottom); Bettmann/Corbis, 26; Topical Press Agency/Getty Images, 28; Mary Evans/Ronald Grant/Everett Collection, 34; Franck Guiziou/Hemis/Corbis, 36; Pat Sutphin/The Post-Register/AP Images, 38; Dale O'Dell/Alamy, 40

CONTENTS

CHAPTER ONE

BEAST IN THE FOREST

High in the forested mountains of Washington State, not far from Ape Canyon, Ruby Ann Easthouse and her family were enjoying a camping trip. They had taken a hike to an overlook.

"Nothing out there but trees," Ruby said to her younger brother, Henry.

The sun was low in the sky as the family turned down the trail back to camp. Night would be falling

Legends about mysterious ape-like creatures exist in cultures around the world.

Bigfoot sightings are common in the forested mountains of the Pacific Northwest.

soon. It was already growing dark under the canopy of trees. Ruby was tired. She lagged behind the others. Then she stopped.

"Hurry up!" Henry called to her. "Never mind," he said to their parents. "I'll go back for her—you go on ahead."

Henry found Ruby staring down at a patch of mud near the trail. "Check this out," she said. "It looks like a footprint!" She shined her flashlight down on the ground. There was a clear outline of what looked like a human footprint. It had large toes. More footprints led off the trail in the direction of a bog.

"Wow, you're right," Henry whispered. "These are footprints. But they're huge! Do you think it's a bear?"

Suddenly they both heard an eerie noise. It sounded like a whistle or a shriek. A strange and awful smell filled the air. The children froze in

Bigfoot's Cousins

Many other varieties of unidentified ape-like creatures have been reported around the world. One is the so-called Skunk Ape. People frequently claim to have spotted this smelly ape in Florida swamps. On the island of Sumatra in Indonesia, another legend describes an unknown primate called the *orang pendek*. This mysterious animal is much shorter than a typical Bigfoot. The orang pendek reportedly stands between two and a half and five feet (0.8–1.5 m) tall.

fear. They looked into the trees in the direction of the sound. In the dim light, they could make out the shape of a huge body. It looked much too large to be a bear.

The creature took a step forward. As the last bits of light shone through the trees, Ruby and Henry could see the creature more clearly. This was no bear. Its head was dome-shaped like a gorilla's. Its body was covered in dark fur. Terrified, the children did not wait another moment. They bolted away as fast as they could.

A Great Ape?

Ruby and Henry's story is only fiction. But it represents many similar tales about a humanlike ape. This mysterious creature is said to dwell in the rugged mountains, dense timber, and deserted swamplands of the United States and Canada. Native Americans have many names for it. The most commonly known is *Sasquatch,* which comes from a Salish Indian word meaning "wild man."

Stories about the beast are found elsewhere all around the globe. In the Himalayas, the Sherpa people of Nepal and Tibet have legends about a large, hairy beast that walks on two legs. They call the animal *yeti,* a term meaning "rock-bear." In Russia and Mongolia, the creature is known as *Almas.* In Scotland, tales are told about *Am Fear Liath Mòr,* or "Gray Man." Chinese people tell of the *Yeren,* which means "wild man." In Australia, people call it a Yowie. To many who follow the oversize tracks of this legend, the mysterious creature is known simply as Bigfoot.

Cryptozoology

Bigfoot is not officially recognized by modern science. However, some scientists study animals whose existence has not been proven. The study of animals that have not yet been discovered is called cryptozoology. The animals studied by cryptozoologists are known as cryptids. These are animals that may or may not exist. Cryptozoologists who study Bigfoot look for evidence, such as hair and footprints.

CHAPTER TWO

IDENTIFYING BIGFOOT AND YETI

Legends about Bigfoot, yeti, and other similar creatures appear in many different cultures around the world. Some of these tales go back thousands of years. Today, people continue to report seeing these animals.

Physical Appearance

People describe Bigfoot and its relatives as looking like an ape but walking upright like a human.

From the descriptions in stories and reported sightings, people can create a possible picture of Bigfoot's appearance and behavior.

Bigfoot by Height

Reports of Bigfoot indicate it could be as tall as 10 to 12 feet (3–3.7 m). The graphic above shows the estimated height of Bigfoot compared with other known mammals. How does the height of Bigfoot compare with the other animals on this chart? Are there any other similarities between these animals and Bigfoot?

This description would make it a primate. Primates are a group of mammals that includes apes, monkeys, and humans. In the United States and Canada, Bigfoot is said to be 7 to 12 feet (2.1–3.7 m) tall. It is covered with brown or black hair. It has large feet and massive shoulders. Some say the creature has a strong, terrible smell, like that of a dead animal or a skunk.

The yeti of the Himalayan mountains is also described as an ape-like creature walking on two feet like a human. This creature is usually said to be a reddish-brown color. However, a few people have described it as having yellow, grayish-white, or black hair. The yeti is slightly shorter than the North American Bigfoot. Reports put it anywhere from five to ten feet (1.5–3 m) tall. The yeti is also frequently reported to have a skunk-like odor.

Diet and Behavior

Bigfoot is said to be mostly vegetarian, eating roots and wild berries. However, it may also hunt wildlife such as rodents and catch salmon from streams. In the Himalayas, the yeti are believed to be carnivores. They eat small

Monster Magic

In the folklore of many cultures, Sasquatch and yeti are beings with magical abilities. In some legends the creature can change its shape. This may explain why humans do not often see the creatures. If Bigfoot hears a human coming near, it might turn into a common animal, such as a rabbit or a squirrel.

animals native to the mountains, such as marmots. Some say they also kill yaks, large herd animals similar to cows.

In some versions of the legend, Bigfoot is described as a terrifying monster that can capture and eat people. However, most believers say the animal is unlikely to attack humans. It is extremely shy of people.

Bigfoot and yeti are nocturnal creatures. They are most often seen at night. In fact, they are more often heard than seen. Both creatures are said to make grunting, groaning, growling, or

Eyes That Glow

Some who claim to see Bigfoot at night claim it has eyes that glow in the dark. This may sound like science fiction. But glowing eyes, known as eyeshine, actually exist in some animals. The effect is common in many nocturnal animals, including bears, deer, raccoons, cats, and dogs. These animals have a special reflective surface inside their eyes. This surface helps them see better in the dark. When light hits their eyes, it is reflected like a mirror. This reflection gives an animal's eyes an eerie red, yellow, blue, or green glow.

Eyeshine helps nocturnal animals, such as raccoons, see better in the dark.

even whistling noises. Some of these Bigfoot calls have been captured on audiotape.

What Is Bigfoot?

There are many theories about what Bigfoot could be. The simplest explanation is that sightings of Bigfoot are mistakes. Many of the sightings are at night, when human eyes cannot see well. People may spot large bears, which sometimes stand on two feet. These people may think they are seeing Bigfoot or a yeti. Other reports and evidence could be hoaxes.

Footprints are some of the best evidence of Bigfoot's existence, but even footprints can be easily faked.

These are deliberate pranks meant to fool people. For instance, one famous hoaxer named Ray Wallace constructed large wooden feet. He used them to create tracks in the mud that he claimed were from a Bigfoot.

But if Bigfoot is real, what is it? Some believers say the animal could belong to an ancient species of ape called *Gigantopithecus*. This giant ape is known to have lived more than 300,000 years ago in Asia. Based on bones that have been found, the ape was about ten feet (3 m) tall. It weighed a massive

EXPLORE ONLINE

The Web site below contains information about the Bigfoot legend. As you know, every source is different. Compare what you learned about Bigfoot and yeti in this chapter with the information on the Web site. Do you think the author of this book believes Bigfoot is real? Do the authors of this Web site believe the creature is real? How can you tell?

Finding the Wood Ape

www.mycorelibrary.com/bigfoot-and-yeti

1,200 pounds (540 kg). This would match reports of Bigfoot's size.

Some believe the ancient ape crossed over to North America from Asia during the Ice Age. As humans spread across the continent, the apes went deeper into the forests and higher into the mountains. A similar theory holds that Bigfoot is descended from an early relative of human beings, such as the Neanderthal. This could explain why it appears so humanlike.

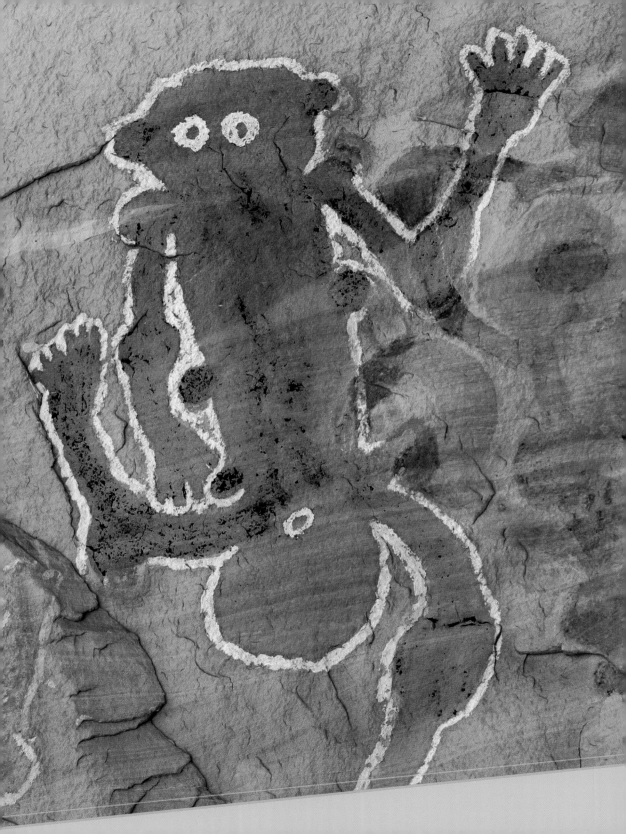

CHAPTER THREE

EARLY SIGHTINGS

Long before Europeans arrived in the Americas, native peoples told stories about giant, hairy, ape-like creatures. Tales about these wild ape-men eventually spread from Native Americans to European settlers.

The earliest published newspaper story about Bigfoot appeared in a New York newspaper, the *Exeter Watchman,* on September 22, 1818. The story

Bigfoot legends go back thousands of years and span the globe. Ancient Aboriginal Australians created rock paintings of Bigfoot-like creatures.

reported the sighting of a "Wild Man of the Woods." According to the story, the creature bent forward when running. It was covered with hair. Footprints were found, showing a narrow heel with spreading toes. After this story was published, more tales of hairy creatures were reported in Indiana, Pennsylvania, and Arkansas.

Bigfoot Attacks

Bigfoot grabbed headlines once again in the early 1900s. In 1924 a group of miners in Washington claimed to see several ape-like creatures. The miners fired shots at them. Later that night, the creatures returned. They threw rocks at the miners' cabin and pounded on the doors while the terrified miners were trapped inside. The attack lasted until morning. The miners left their cabin that day. The incident was reported in the local newspaper, the *Oregonian*. From that time on, the site has been known as Ape Canyon. The incident at Ape Canyon was impossible to verify. But it became part of Bigfoot folklore.

Wild Man of the Snows

The people of the Himalayan mountains have long shared folktales about an ape-like beast. These stories spread to Europe in the 1800s and early 1900s, when explorers first came to the area.

British explorer Lieutenant Colonel C. K. Howard-Bury came to

A Mystery in Stone

Archaeologists have found stone carvings along the Columbia River in Oregon that appear to represent monkey and ape faces. Ape-like creatures have also been depicted in Native-American totem poles, masks, and woven baskets. Some historians find this surprising because there are no monkeys or apes native to North America. Some believers think the stories and pictures might prove Bigfoot once lived among the Native Americans.

As Europeans began exploring the Himalayan mountains, they brought home tales of mysterious, ape-like creatures.

Tibet to climb Mount Everest in 1921. He and his team saw some humanlike footprints in the snow. Howard-Bury thought a gray wolf had likely made them. As the wolf ran, its prints may have overlapped

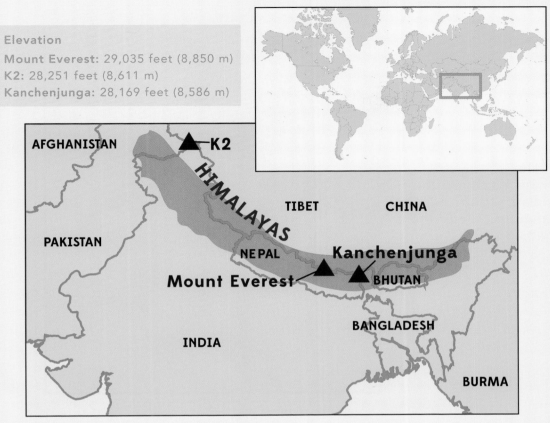

Elevation
Mount Everest: 29,035 feet (8,850 m)
K2: 28,251 feet (8,611 m)
Kanchenjunga: 28,169 feet (8,586 m)

AFGHANISTAN
K2
HIMALAYAS
TIBET
CHINA
PAKISTAN
NEPAL
Kanchenjunga
Mount Everest
BHUTAN
BANGLADESH
INDIA
BURMA

Map of the Himalayan Region

This map shows the Himalayan region. In which countries can the Himalayan mountains be found? Two of the three tallest peaks on Earth are a part of this mountain range. Can you find them on the map? Why might this remote area be a likely habitat for a creature like the yeti?

to make them look larger and more like human prints. But the Tibetan Sherpas insisted *metoh-kangmi*, or "wild men of the snows," had made the prints.

Tales of the yeti have captured the imaginations of people around the world.

British newspaper reporters exaggerated the tale. One reporter mistakenly translated the word *metoh* to mean "abominable," or horrible. He claimed Howard-Bury's team had discovered the "abominable snowman." The colorful phrase caught on in the press. Soon, the fantastic story was front-page news across the globe.

British explorer Laurence Waddell traveled through the Himalayas during the 1880s and 1890s. On one expedition, he discovered mysterious footprints:

> Some large footprints in the snow led across our path, and away up to the higher peaks. These were alleged to be the trail of the hairy wild men who are believed to live amongst the eternal snows, along with the mythical white lions, whose roar is reputed to be heard during storms. The belief in these creatures is universal among Tibetans. None, however, of the many Tibetans I have interrogated on this subject could ever give me an authentic case. On the most superficial investigation it always resolved itself into something that somebody heard tell of. These so-called hairy wild men are evidently the great yellow snow-bear . . . which is highly carnivorous, and often kills yaks.
>
> Source: L. A. Waddell. *Among the Himalayas. Westminster, PA: A. Constable and Co.,* 1900. Print. 223–224.

Changing Minds

In this passage, what does Waddell think is the true source of the footprints? Do you agree with his conclusion? Imagine your best friend has the opposite opinion. Write a few sentences explaining to your friend why you think the footprints were or were not made by a yeti.

CHAPTER FOUR

SEPARATING FACT FROM FICTION

During the 1950s and 1960s, the legend of the ape-man became a bigger sensation than ever. Newspaper reporters, scientists, and explorers focused their attention on one question: Is Bigfoot real?

Quest for the Yeti

In 1951 British mountaineer Eric Shipton discovered a large footprint in the snows of the Himalayas. Shipton

A hunter measures a possible Bigfoot print in Oregon in 1971.

Eric Shipton laid an ice ax alongside the strange print he found to show its huge size.

photographed the print and sent it to newspapers. The photo created a lot of excitement. Many people believed it could only be the footprint of a yeti.

The race was on to find the abominable snowman. Over the next ten years, many teams of mountain climbers set off for the Himalayan mountains. They hoped to capture, or at least photograph, a yeti. In 1954 the London newspaper

Daily Mail sponsored an expedition to find the beast. Texas millionaire Tom Slick launched his own hunt in 1957. The following year, a Russian team attempted to find the yeti. The best-known expedition took place in 1960. Famous mountain climber Sir Edmund Hillary led the expedition.

None of the teams caught a glimpse of the yeti. However, they did uncover some yeti artifacts. These very old remains, including a hand, skins, and several scalps, had been kept in Buddhist monasteries in Nepal. The monks believed they were from yeti.

Scientists analyzed hair from the scalps and skins. One scalp was

Mysterious Tracks

Mysterious footprints often turn out to have a simple explanation. For instance, prints from two different animals may overlap, making the tracks look unusually large and strange. Prints from the front and back paws of a bear can overlap as the animal runs. This can leave large tracks that may look like those of a Bigfoot. Tracks made in snow may change and grow larger as the snow melts around them.

Sir Edmund Hillary, right, and Sherpa Khunjo Chumb, left, examine what might be a yeti scalp in 1960.

found to be made from the hide of a rare, goat-like animal called a *serow*. The skins were from a Tibetan blue bear. The yeti hand remained a mystery for many years. In 2011 DNA testing on a finger from the yeti hand showed the finger was from a human, not a yeti. However, these findings did not stop people from believing in the yeti.

Bigfoot in the Spotlight

While explorers searched the remote Himalayas for evidence of the yeti, Bigfoot made an appearance in the United States. In 1958 workers were building a road near Willow Creek, California. One day they found large footprints around their site. The prints appeared to have been made by a humanlike creature. But they were a startling 16 inches (41 cm) long. One of the workers made plaster casts of the footprints. They were shown in newspapers. People said the prints must have been made by a "Bigfoot." The name stuck. Over the next several years, many other prints were reported in Washington, Oregon, and western Canada.

Then, in 1967, Bigfoot researcher Roger Patterson made an exciting announcement. He had caught Bigfoot on film! Patterson claimed he and his friend Bob Gimlin had spotted the Bigfoot while horseback riding in Bluff Creek, California. The strange creature was sitting beside a creek. Patterson filmed the animal as it walked away into the trees. The video seems to show a female ape, more than six feet (1.8 m) tall. She is covered with black hair.

Skeptics say the animal looks like a man in a fur suit. However, many believers claim the Patterson-Gimlin film is the best evidence yet that Bigfoot exists.

In 2011 a *National Geographic* team traveled to Tibet to find evidence of the yeti. The team interviewed a woman who said she was attacked by a yeti in the 1970s. Lhakpa Dolma claimed to have been tending her yak herd when the yeti appeared:

> *Suddenly, the yeti hit me from behind like a hammer and grabbed my neck. It lifted and dropped a cow. It gouged a wound in the side until the blood flowed. It sucked out all the blood. Then it took a baby cow and dropped it against the rock and drunk its blood. The calf didn't die. The yeti left. . . . The teeth were big. It had a wrinkled face, the eyes were sunk in deep. It walked like this, but very fast. The skin on the hands were cracked, and the nails were very long.*
>
> Source: "Hunt for the Abominable Snowman." National Geographic. National Geographic Society, 2013. Web. Accessed August 29, 2013.

Nice View

After reading the text above, go back and reread the passage by explorer Laurence Waddell in Chapter Three. Does Lhakpa Dolma's report about the yeti match what Waddell heard from his Tibetan guides? Does Lhakpa Dolma's story fit with the most common versions of the legend you've read about in this book? Write a short paragraph comparing Lhakpa Dolma's view of the yeti with that of other legends in the book.

CHAPTER FIVE

THE LEGEND CONTINUES

Stories about Bigfoot and yeti continue to fascinate people. Bigfoot has made appearances in many books, movies, and TV shows. The reality television show *Finding Bigfoot* follows a team of real-life Bigfoot hunters, the Bigfoot Field Researchers Organization (BFRO).

In the Himalayas, the yeti is a popular image. It has appeared on its own postage stamp in the country

In the 1987 movie Harry and the Hendersons, a Bigfoot finds a home with a US family.

Yeti Airlines transports tourists—and yeti hunters—to the Himalayas.

of Bhutan. In Nepal, tourists can fly on Yeti Airlines and stay at a hotel called the Yak and Yeti. Even though nobody has ever proven that these creatures exist, people seem eager to believe in the legend.

New Discoveries

Every day, people still report seeing Bigfoot, hearing its calls, or finding its footprints or hair. Several Web sites collect firsthand accounts of sightings. In September 2000, the BFRO captured headlines with an unusual discovery—a Bigfoot body print. The print was found in a muddy spot in Skookum Meadows, Washington. From the imprint, the creature appeared to be lying down and reaching for some fruit. A plaster cast was made of the body print.

Anthropologist Jeff Meldrum of Idaho State University analyzed the cast. He thought it showed a clear outline of a Sasquatch's heel. Other scientists thought the imprint was probably from an elk. Hairs stuck to the cast were analyzed. Some of them were from elk and some from a

Real-Life Hobbits?

In 2003 scientists made an incredible discovery on the island of Flores in Indonesia. They found bones from a new species of human, which they called *Homo floresiensis*. When they examined the fossils, scientists estimated the people lived about 12,000 years ago. They were tiny compared to *Homo sapiens*, our species. Scientists nicknamed them "hobbits" because of their small size. The discovery of real-life hobbits gave Bigfoot researchers hope. Someday, the bones of a Bigfoot may be found!

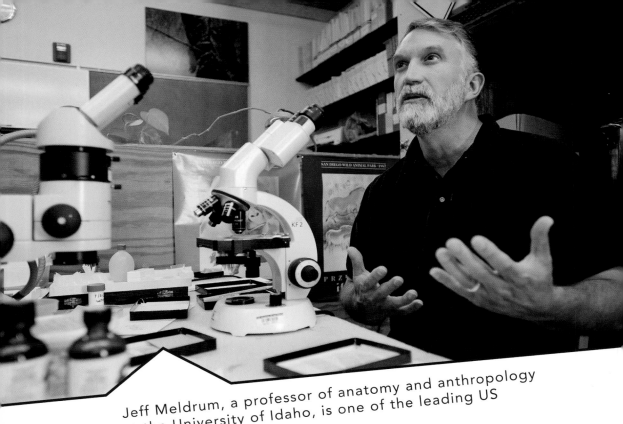

Jeff Meldrum, a professor of anatomy and anthropology at the University of Idaho, is one of the leading US Bigfoot researchers.

bear. Others hairs could not be identified. Several scientists have argued that the hairs could be from an unknown primate.

In 2012 researchers from Switzerland and the United Kingdom began a new study called the Oxford-Lausanne Hominid Project. They invited people to send in hair, bones, and other artifacts believed to be from Bigfoot, yeti, or similar unknown creatures. Scientists planned to analyze the DNA found in these specimens. This will help scientists determine each artifact's origins. If the DNA found is unrecognized, it may lead to the discovery of a new species.

A Legend Lives On

Does Bigfoot or any of its relatives truly exist today? No one has found evidence to prove Bigfoot's existence yet. Scientists need to examine the creature itself, or at least some of its bones or body parts, in order to confirm that it exists. But Bigfoot searchers are still on the hunt. They hope

In Search of New Species

Discovering a brand-new species of primate may sound far-fetched. But many Bigfoot believers point to other new species that have been found in modern times. The coelacanth, an ancient species of fish, was thought to have been extinct for 60 million years. But it was found living in South Africa in 1938. Most Americans had never seen a giant panda until 1937 when one was captured in China and brought to a zoo. In 1992 a new species of ox was discovered living in Vietnam and Laos.

Cryptozoologists can use heat-sensing cameras to help find mysterious creatures.

new technologies, such as heat sensors, night-vision glasses, and motion-detecting cameras, can help capture evidence of the beast.

Other believers, including many Native Americans and Tibetans, do not need hard evidence.

FURTHER EVIDENCE

Chapter Five gives a picture of how the legend of Bigfoot and yeti continues today. What is the main point of this chapter? What key evidence supports this point? Visit the Web site below for more information about the Bigfoot legend. Find a quote from the Web site that supports this chapter's main point. Does the quote support an existing piece of evidence in the chapter? Or does it add a new one?

Bigfoot Encounters

www.mycorelibrary.com/bigfoot-and-yeti

They accept the legends and stories handed down from their ancestors. In the end, Bigfoot may or may not be a real, living animal. But one thing is certain: its legend is very much alive.

Sasquatch or Bigfoot

United States and Canada

Native peoples of the United States and Canada have long told stories about a "wild man" commonly known as Sasquatch or Bigfoot. The creature is said to be 7 to 12 feet (2.1–3.7 m) tall and covered in hair.

Yowie

Australia

According to legends told by native peoples in Australia, the Yowie is an ape-like or humanlike monster. It walks on two legs and is covered with hair. It has extremely long arms and its feet point backward. The Yowie is between 7 and 12 feet (2.1–3.7 m) tall.

Almas

Mongolia

The *Almas,* which means "wild man" in Mongolian, is a humanlike creature, more like a wild human than an ape. Often seen in the mountain ranges of Central Asia and Mongolia, it is said to walk on two legs and is covered with reddish-brown hair.

Orang Pendek

Indonesia

The orang pendek (Indonesian for "short person") is a small ape-like creature said to live on the Indonesian island of Sumatra. It is covered in hair and stands between two and a half and five feet (0.8–1.5 m) tall. Some say it has feet that point backward.

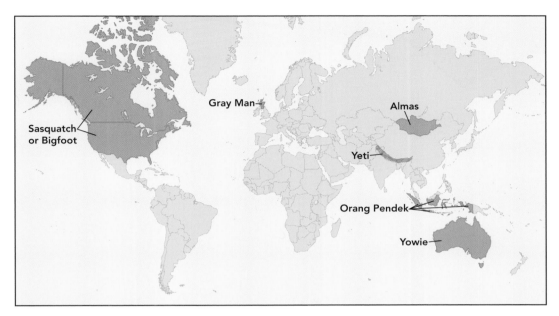

Gray Man
Sasquatch or Bigfoot
Almas
Yeti
Orang Pendek
Yowie

Gray Man

Scotland

The Gray Man, or *Am Fear Liath Mòr*, is a mysterious creature said to live in the mountains of Scotland. The Gray Man stands up to 20 feet (6.1 m) tall and is covered in gray or brown hair. It has the power to control the fog and create deep fear in humans.

Yeti

Himalayas

The yeti is an ape-like creature dwelling high in the Himalayan mountains. It is covered in reddish-brown, yellow, grayish-white, or black hair. It is slightly shorter than the North American Bigfoot, at about five to ten feet (1.5–3 m) tall.

Why Do I Care?

According to the Bigfoot Field Researchers Organization (BFRO), Bigfoot has been spotted in nine Canadian provinces and in every US state except Hawaii. The BFRO collects reports of these encounters on its Web site. Many other Web sites collect similar reports. With an adult's help, go online and look up some of these reports. Have any Sasquatch sightings been reported in your area?

Say What?

Studying the legend and science of Bigfoot can mean learning a lot of new vocabulary. Find five words in this book that you've never heard before. Use a dictionary or the glossary to find out what they mean. Then write the meanings in your own words, and use each word in a new sentence.

Surprise Me

After reading this book, what two or three facts about Bigfoot and yeti did you find most surprising? Write a few sentences about each fact. Why did you find them surprising?

You Are There

This book describes several stories about encounters with Bigfoot and yeti. Use your imagination to write your own story about Bigfoot. Put yourself in the place of an explorer in search of Bigfoot. In your story, describe the tools you take with you to help you find the creature. Tell how you look for it, and what evidence you find.

GLOSSARY

abominable
very bad; hateful

anthropologist
a scientist who studies human beings

cryptid
a creature that has not yet been discovered and may or may not exist

cryptozoology
the study of creatures that have not yet been discovered by modern science

DNA
material found in animal cells that is handed down from parents to children

hoax
a deliberate prank meant to fool people

nocturnal
most active at night

Sherpas
native people who live in the Himalayan mountains of Nepal and Tibet; they are expert mountain climbers

skeptic
a person who is doubtful of something's existence

species
a group of living things that share certain characteristics

LEARN MORE

Books

Halls, Kelly Milner. *In Search of Sasquatch*. New York: Houghton Mifflin Harcourt, 2011.

Hamilton, Sue L. *Monsters*. Edina, MN: ABDO, 2007.

Theisen, Paul. *Bigfoot*. Minneapolis: Bellwether, 2011.

Web Links

To learn more about Bigfoot and the yeti, visit ABDO Publishing Company online at **www.abdopublishing.com**. Web sites about Bigfoot and the yeti are featured on our Book Links page. These links are routinely monitored and updated to provide the most current information available.

Visit **www.mycorelibrary.com** for free additional tools for teachers and students.

INDEX

ABOUT THE AUTHOR

Jennifer Joline Anderson has been writing since she was a teenager, when she won an award and had a story published in *Seventeen* magazine. She lives in Minneapolis, Minnesota, with her husband and two children.